Original title:
The Happiness of Christmas Giving

Copyright © 2024 Creative Arts Management OÜ
All rights reserved.

Author: Evelyn Hartman
ISBN HARDBACK: 978-9916-94-020-4
ISBN PAPERBACK: 978-9916-94-021-1

Kindness in Every Package

A box of socks, a bobblehead,
Wrapped in tape, but love instead.
A fruitcake lodged in festive cheer,
Who knew that gifts could bring a sneer?

A sweater three sizes too tight,
A candle that just won't ignite.
Yet laughter echoes in a blink,
As we unwrap with frantic pink!

The Spirit of Generosity

A box of joy tied with a bow,
Inside a rubber chicken, who'd know?
We giggle as we trade our loot,
With silly hats and mismatched boots.

A gift that squeaks and wobbles too,
The kind of joy that's tried and true.
Not always perfect, but that's fine,
In each odd gift, our smiles align!

Wrapped in Love's Embrace

A cactus wrapped in fluffy fluff,
It pricks my heart, but that's enough.
A card with doodles, cats and dogs,
Together we laugh at our silly fogs.

A homemade sweater with one arm,
Not quite my size, but full of charm.
Each quirky gift, a loving tease,
Brings laughter, joy, and endless peace!

Whispers of Winter Kindness

A snow globe filled with jelly beans,
A quirky gift from crazy dreams.
We trade our cards with glue and pasta,
Making memories, oh what a blast-a!

A gift of socks with silly prints,
That makes us laugh until it hints.
With each surprise, our hearts still grow,
In this wild cheer, goodwill will flow!

Infusing Light into Shadows

In the attic, lights are tangled,
A cat's tail is now in a jangle.
Try to hang them, what a sight,
A Christmas tree with a feisty fight.

With every ornament that's hung,
Someone sings a carol wrong.
Laughter echoes through the cheer,
As the cat claims the topmost sphere.

The Art of Giving

Gifts wrapped up in newspaper old,
With bows made from yarn, not gold.
A surprise inside, what can it be?
Oh look! A sock! That's just for me.

Handmade cards with glitter spread,
Getting stuck to a brother's head.
Each gift a joy wrapped with flair,
Forgetting to check what's in my chair!

Love's Embrace in a Snowy World

Snowflakes falling, oh what fun,
Sledding down the hill, here we run!
A snowball fight erupts with glee,
But someone just got struck by me.

Building snowmen, big and round,
One has lost its eyes, oh, how profound!
It melts away with laughter loud,
As we sit together, feeling proud.

Glistening Moments of Togetherness

Cookies baked and burnt a bit,
Flour on faces, every skit.
The kitchen's chaos, flour in air,
Mom yells, 'Find the milk, if you dare!'

Board games played with too much spice,
Someone lands on Santa, oh so nice.
With giggles and cheers, we play our part,
Each round a bump to the merry heart.

Warm Hugs in the Winter Chill

Snowflakes dance in frosty air,
Jolly folks with gifts to share.
Socks for toes, a silly hat,
Laughter echoes, 'A cat? A bat?'

Gifts wrapped tight, but dogs still gnaw,
Mom's new slippers now have flaws.
Santa slips, a funny sight,
Spreading joy on this cold night.

Beneath the Stars

Under twinkling lights we cheer,
Sipping cocoa, it's the best time of year.
A reindeer dressed in a sparkly tie,
Neighbor shouts, 'No way to fly!'

Christmas trees with extra flair,
Elves dancing without a care.
Snowball fights all through the street,
'Take that!' as his mittens meet his feet.

Hearts Unite

Cookies baked with too much spice,
'Just a pinch'—that advice was nice!
Frosting on the dog, what a treat,
Christmas cheer can't be beat!

Grab a sweater, one too tight,
Look at those lights—what a sight!
Friends all gather, share a joke,
Out pops a clown with a funny cloak.

Candles of Hope in the Darkness

Candles flicker, shadows dance,
Grandpa snorts at the cat's prance.
Somehow someone said 'more pie!'
All agree—it's worth the try!

Laughter bubbles when gifts go wrong,
Uncle Bob sings his favorite song.
What's that smell? Did someone sneeze?
Oh dear, open all the windows, please!

Treasures of the Heart

Box of trinkets, bright and bold,
A rubber chicken, tales retold.
Mom's homemade sweater, looks so fine,
But wait—are those sleeves made for a pine?

Stars are twinkling, dogs wear bows,
Snowmen fall when the wind blows.
Gather round, the stories start,
Laughter's the treasure, and it warms the heart.

Wrapped in Warmth

Snowflakes dance upon my nose,
While dad wears reindeer clothes.
A gift that's wrapped but not quite right,
Is actually mom's fruitcake fright.

Hot cocoa spills on Christmas eve,
I swear it's not the mugs that weave.
An awkward hug from grandma near,
And suddenly it's all too clear!

Beyond Borders

From grandma's jam to uncle's cheese,
These gifts contain more than just fees.
A travel mug for sour tea,
Who knew their humor matched with glee?

Pasta shaped like Christmas trees,
Not quite sure how to say 'cheese'.
Wrapped up in laughter, gifts galore,
Beyond borders, we love to explore!

A Heartfelt Season of Togetherness

The dog's in headgear, quite a sight,
Tinsel sticking to his bite.
Mom says calm down, let them breathe,
While dad sneezes—it's just a wreath!

With cousins singing off-key notes,
And snickering at silly quotes.
Together we laugh, we dance, we sing,
In joy, the cheer this season brings.

The Glow of Giving Hearts

Candles flicker, shadows play,
I tripped on the lights—what a display!
A present's wrapped like a giant pie,
But it's just old socks, oh my, oh my!

With cookies shaped into strange forms,
We share a giggle as warmth warms.
In giving we find the brightest cheer,
Laughter's the gift we hold so dear.

Bright Stars and Brighter Souls

Under bright stars, we make a toast,
To that fruitcake—to be honest, the worst!
Handmade crafts that rival a pro,
Adventures await, just follow the glow.

With silly hats and funny charms,
We gather near with open arms.
The glow of spirits, wild and free,
In every heart lies the best glee!

Laughter Beneath the Mistletoe

A cat in a hat, what a sight,
Trying to dance, oh what a fright!
The dog's stealing cookies, it's all in good fun,
While grandma's still searching for the last bun.

With ribbons and bows all over the place,
Uncle Joe trips, oh what a disgrace!
The kids start to giggle, it's all a big mess,
But laughter fills rooms, it's more than a guess.

Embracing the Spirit of Sharing

A sweater too bright worn with pride,
Thought it was a gift, but it's really a ride!
We share funny stories, with tea on the side,
Even a turkey that seems to have lied.

A pie in the oven, the smoke starts to rise,
Dad says it's gourmet, but oh what a disguise!
With giggles and grins, the laughter won't cease,
As we toast to the moments, which never decrease.

Brightening Hearts on Frosty Nights

The snowman is crooked, but we don't really care,
He wears mom's old scarf and a wig made of hair.
With cocoa in hand, we burst out with glee,
As snowflakes fall softly, right down on our spree.

Hearts glow like lights on the tallest of trees,
While grandpa recites, "Just pass me the cheese!"
With twinkling eyes and laughter so bright,
We celebrate together, this frosty delight.

Symbols of Love and Kindness

A jingle of bells, what's that sound?
It's cousin Pat's dance with a sandwich he found!
Gifts wrapped in paper, some mismatched and torn,
Still, smiles abound since this love was reborn.

With hugs and with giggles, we gather around,
You'd think we were clowns, oh what joy we have found!

Sharing our quirks with the love that we send,
In this wild little world, we'll always be friends.

Hand-in-Hand through Winter's Wonderland

Snowflakes dance like little sprites,
As we stroll under twinkling lights.
With mittens thick and noses pink,
We share hot cocoa, and giggle, I think.

Snowmen frown with carrot noses,
While we laugh at all their poses.
Rolling snowballs, aiming, oh dear!
Hit the neighbor, and we cheer!

Stories of Generosity by the Fire

By the fire, our tales unfold,
Of gifts wrapped tight, and friends so bold.
A cat with tinsel in its sight,
Knocked down the tree, oh what a fright!

We chuckle at socks, mismatched and bright,
Each pair a treasure for sheer delight.
Grandma knitted with love, oh yes!
Too big, but it's still a warm caress!

A Tapestry of Thoughtful Gifts

Boxing day brings mystery and glee,
What's inside? A dance for me!
A fruitcake that weighs like a stone,
Yet I still take it, none can moan.

With bows that stick in hair, oh no!
Presents gone rogue, in a wild show.
Laughter fills the room so bright,
As we unwrap joy with all our might.

Sealed with a Smile

Gift exchanges with goofy grins,
Lifesavers, candies, and rubber chickens!
Taped up boxes that might just burst,
Each surprise, we take, then rehearse.

A sweater for Dad that's way too tight,
A bobblehead that gives him fright.
Yet laughter echoes, as friends unite,
Sealed with a smile, what pure delight!

Echoes of Joyful Hearts

In a world of wrapping paper,
We dance with scotch tape in hand.
A gift that's just a little lumpy,
Leaves us giggling, oh so grand.

Shiny bows that twist in knots,
Our cats think it's a jungle gym.
With every cheer and every laugh,
We're loving this holiday whim.

The kitchen's chaos from the feast,
Turkey's burnt but spirits soar.
As we toast with apple cider,
Who needs perfection? Just want more!

Even when the lights go dim,
And carols turn to playful night.
We find joy in silly shenanigans,
Creating memories, oh what a sight!

The Gift of Giving Time

Rushed around, oh what a sight,
Forgot the gift? That's all right.
A hug wrapped in a cheerful grin,
Is worth much more than where you've been.

Ten shopping lists and none complete,
Yet laughter fills the crowded street.
'It's the thought,' we say with glee,
While dodging carts and sipping tea.

Cookies burned and laughter shared,
The charm is found in how we cared.
Board games spread, competitive cheer,
Best gift's the fun that's always here.

So here's to time, a priceless win,
The jokes, the love, where we begin.
Forget the stress, with all our might,
We'll gift pure joy this merry night!

Heartstrings Tied with Ribbons

Tangled lights and ribbons bright,
Add our giggles to the night.
With each present under the tree,
A little chaos sets us free.

In the corner, dog wears a hat,
As we laugh, he gives a pat.
Grandma's fruitcake, oh what a treat,
It wobbles like a dancing feet!

We wrap our hearts with laughter strong,
In every note, we sing along.
A warmth that's felt, both near and far,
In the silliness, we find the star.

So here's to joy, imperfect and bright,
With heartstrings tight, we hold on tight.
For every chuckle, every cheer,
Makes this season the best time of year!

Laughter Beneath the Mistletoe

Beneath the sprigs of green delight,
A game of kisses, oh what a sight!
Who's brave enough to take the chance,
For a peck or two in a merry dance?

Each joke shared under twinkling lights,
Turns us giddy on cold nights.
With cups of cocoa, and silly games,
We embrace the joy that still remains.

Frosty smiles and playful shoves,
In this spirit, we share our loves.
As wrapping paper flies through the air,
We find the fun, it's everywhere.

So raise your mugs, let laughter ring,
In moments simple, hear joy sing.
Beneath the mistletoe's brave show,
We find the gifts that truly glow!

Embracing the Cheerful Flurry

Snowflakes dance, oh so spry,
With mittens on, we laugh and try.
Gifts wrapped tight in paper bold,
Unraveling secrets, tales of old.

Giggles burst like jingle bells,
Hot cocoa spills, oh how it smells!
We tangle lights, what a sight,
A glowing mess, but feels just right.

Carols sung in off-key notes,
As we warm our chilly throats.
Santa's sleigh, a bumpy ride,
Full of cheer we cannot hide.

Share the jokes and silly hats,
Baking cookies; oh, the chats!
Laughter echoes, echoed bright,
In this flurry, hearts take flight.

Sparkles of Compassion

A gift for you, a sock, a shoe,
What else could I possibly do?
But giggle when I see your face,
This sparkly joy, our little race.

Twinkling lights adorn the tree,
Reflecting love and mischief, see?
I wrapped your gift, a laughter flare,
It's just a rock, but we don't care!

Neighbors cozy by the fire,
Sipping tea, our hearts aspire.
A holiday toast, oh what a trend,
To silly moments that never end.

Handmade cards with doodles bright,
A stick figure in snow, what a sight!
Each giggle shared, a treasure found,
In sparkles of joy, we're tightly bound.

Threads of Warmth and Wonder

Stitch by stitch, we weave our cheer,
A scarf for you, a smile to wear.
Oh, the tangled yarn we fight,
Yet giggles tangle, oh what a sight!

Baking cookies, oh what a mess,
Flour on faces, I must confess.
A sprinkle here and a dollop there,
Tasting dough with silly flair.

Stockings hung without a care,
Filled with goodies, plus a bear!
Silly notes that make no sense,
This joy we share is so immense.

Gifts of laughter, hugs in tow,
In knit and purl, our love will grow.
The warmth we share, it's truly grand,
In threads of wonder, hand in hand.

Yuletide Serenity

Oh, the peace of winter's brew,
Mismatched gloves but hearts so true.
We sip our cider, warm and sweet,
    Juliet's cat steals the treat!

Holiday cards all go to fluff,
We scribble jokes; it's all enough.
Neighbors stop, they drop their cares,
Strangers laugh, a pet parade shares.

Wishing frosty friends a cheer,
With sloppy snowmen to endear.
A snowball fight, let's clear the lane,
With chilly glee, we dance in rain!

In our hearts, the fun resides,
With every gift, our joy abides.
Yuletide warmth, a bright embrace,
In laughter's joy, we find our place.

Cherished Moments in Frosty Air

With scarves and mittens, we dash outside,
Snowballs fly as we giggle and glide,
Elves in the park, they're laughing so loud,
Reindeer have joined, oh what a crowd!

The cocoa's hot, but spills on your shoe,
You laugh it off, as only friends do,
In a snowman's hat, we find a pet cat,
It sneezes so loud, oh where's the mat?

We sing carols wrong, but who even cares?
The neighbor's dog joins, adding to our flares,
With twinkling lights, we dance on the street,
In frosty air where joy and mischief meet.

Footsteps in snow, we leave silly trails,
Chasing each other, with giggles and wails,
Under the moon, we create a ruckus,
In moments of laughter, what could be luckus?

Celebrating Connection in Every Corner

In every store, the crowd's quite a sight,
With shopping carts bumping, chaos takes flight,
A tangle of tinsel and lights in your hair,
You smile at the chaos, you've got enough flair.

The food's all a-drip, your plate's an art show,
With pie on your shirt, you still steal the show,
Neighbors all shout, in their holiday cheer,
Through laughter and mess, we hold each other near.

A handful of gifts, wrapped crooked and tight,
You hand me a sweater — it's four sizes right,
Yet still, we embrace with laughter and glee,
For moments like these are the best recipe.

The lights that we string are surely a test,
For a tangle of garlands wraps up like a nest,
Still, we untie, laughing with each little fight,
For in every corner, the joy feels just right.

Love's Journey on a Snowy Path

We trudge through the snow, with pockets of cheer,
A slip on the ice brings a giggle so near,
Your mittens are bright, my boots are a mess,
But hand in hand, we embrace the cold stress.

As sleigh bells jingle, we hop on the ride,
A squirrel steals snacks, oh what a wild slide,
We spill our hot drinks, it's a flavorful fight,
But in this shenanigan, everything's bright.

In moments of warmth, under blankets we snuggle,
When a snowball's thrown, our laughter will bubble,
With cheeks all flushed, a scene so enticing,
In snowy adventures, our hearts are so icing.

Side by side, we sing, slightly off-key,
With colds on our noses — pure harmony,
In a world wrapped in frost, we find our own way,
Through love's little journey, the fun's here to stay.

Silhouettes of Joy Against the Snow

Against the white, our shadows do dance,
With snowflakes swirling, we spin in a trance,
Sleds fly down hills with a comedic might,
While tumbling down, we land in delight.

In hot chocolate bars, the marshmallows fly,
You toss one at me, oh me, oh my!
The laughter ricochets, like jingle-bell tunes,
In joyful collisions, our spirit just balloons.

We craft our weird snowman, with a carrot that's lost,
He wobbles and tilts, oh at what a cost,
With a smile so silly and mismatched clothes,
In moments like these, our true laughter glows.

As stars start to shine through the crisp frosty sky,
We cheer to the night, with a wink and a sigh,
In silhouettes bright, joy against the blue,
In the laughter of winter, I cherish you too.

Joy Wrapped in Favors

In a box, I wrapped my cat,
With a note that said, 'Please don't spat!'
Though she leaped and then did pout,
I'm sure she'll get a laugh, no doubt.

Cookies baked with care, but wait!
I mistook salt for sugar, mate!
Friends will laugh till they can't stand,
When they bite and find my blunder bland.

A hat made of fruit loops I designed,
Worn by Dad, he looked quite blind!
We snapped a pic, what a sight!
This season brings both joy and fright.

Wrapping paper mixed with tape,
My gifts now look like some odd shape.
Still, smiles bloom like flowers bright,
As laughter fills our cozy night.

Gifts of Warmth and Light

I bought a sweater, one size fits all,
But it looks like a circus tent, quite tall!
Grandma wore it, such a sight!
We laughed till tears shone bright.

Jars of jam with labels grand,
But they're actually pickles, wasn't planned!
A friend's face went from joy to cries,
As he tasted my surprise disguise.

A DIY card made of my old socks,
With doodles of cats, but mostly rocks.
Everyone loves my art so wild,
Though I'm sure it's not what they'd filed.

Each gift is wrapped in giggles and cheer,
Even when the outcomes aren't clear.
We may stumble, but hearts will ignite,
As we share this warm, joyful light.

A Season of Sharing Smiles

With a snowman made of mashed potatoes,
I served it to guests, their jaw at low rates!
Their laughter echoed throughout the home,
As the furry dog tried to roam.

A mystery box of socks and tape,
Friends unwrapped it, what a shape!
Laughter roared as they dug inside,
To find a rubber chicken, what a ride!

Deck the halls with all things bright,
But forgot garland, so I used a kite.
We flew it high, amidst the glee,
As it swirled in the bright, festive spree.

Holiday tunes that sing off-key,
Yet we dance as if we're royalty.
No perfect gifts, just friends with style,
In this wacky season, we share a smile.

Beneath the Twinkling Stars

Beneath the stars, our carols rise,
While Uncle Joe attempts surprise!
His dancing moves, a sight so poor,
Yet, we laugh and shout for more!

Mismatched socks for all, I declared,
As we unwrapped, each laughed, and stared.
"Best present ever!" a cousin proclaimed,
While I wondered how I got so blamed.

The Christmas tree's a sight to see,
With ornaments made by all but me.
A spaghetti strand, a paper plate,
My friends can't breathe, they stick out late!

Under the glow of twinkling lights,
We giggle, dancing through the nights.
With laughter as our merry guide,
We find joy is always inside.

Threads of Kindness Weaving Together

With gifts of socks and quirky hats,
A reindeer dance with silly chats.
When socks don't match, we cheer and grin,
The joy of giving's where we win.

Old sweaters wrapped with love in mind,
A prize inside, what will we find?
A note that says, 'I'm really neat!'
A Christmas laugh, a silly treat.

A potted plant that may not thrive,
Yet love makes that old cacti jive.
We're threading joy with every stitch,
In laughter's fabric, all is rich.

Tangled lights and ornaments bright,
Facial hair made of snowball fright.
With cheer we string our hearts along,
In this wild world, we all belong.

A Time for Giving, A Time for Love

A gift that squeaks, that's quite a find,
Wrapped twice just to blow your mind.
Mismatched bows and sticky tape,
It's chaos wrapped, but who needs cape?

A fancy mug that's really swell,
With coffee grounds, that's just as well.
And fruitcake too, that only lasts,
For two short days, then it's all past.

A pair of mittens, one is lost,
Included love, but at what cost?
Yet laughter makes the best of these,
A kooky smile that's sure to please.

So gather round, share silly cheer,
For all the fun that brings us near.
A great big hug, now that's the goal,
We jingle joy right to our soul.

Snowflakes and Kindness Fall

Snowflakes landing on our nose,
A friendly shove, and off we go!
To build a snowman, tall and spry,
With carrot hats, oh me, oh my!

A pie that looks like foot instead,
An arch of laughter, joy widespread.
With sprinkles, cherries, oh so bright,
It's cheer and fun, a sweet delight.

A jolly hat from Grandpa's chest,
With silly patterns, he was the best.
We wear them out, so every eye
Sees humor's light, beneath the sky.

As snowflakes fall, we dance around,
In laughter's grip, our hearts are bound.
From random joy, we're never done,
For kindness sprouts and sprinkles fun!

The Melodies of Generous Spirits

With jingle bells that play off-key,
Oh dear, what's that? A melody!
The cats are howling, dogs are too,
In harmony, just me and you.

We gift our friends with socks so bright,
They giggle loud; what a great sight!
The joy we bring, a song so sweet,
A silly dance, and oh, how fleet!

Old records spin with silly cheer,
A welcomed sound that draws us near.
We laugh until we're in a heap,
These tunes of love, forever keep.

When spirits soar through every note,
In giving, laughing, we take the boat.
The waves of joy are loud and clear,
In melodies true, let's spread good cheer!

Festive Rhythms of Connection

In the kitchen, cookies stick,
Grandma's dance—a wobbly trick.
Uncle's hat—too big, it slips,
Nothing beats our laughter trips.

Snowflakes tumble, all around,
Sledding races, leaps abound.
Hot cocoa spills, oh what fun,
With each sip, we all are one.

Songs sung off-key, merry cheer,
Voices blend, the joy is clear.
With reindeer games and silly cheer,
We spread our love far and near.

Each gift wrapped with giggles tight,
Mismatched socks in morning light.
In this season, we all bring,
Joyful tunes, let laughter sing.

A Lantern of Love in Winter's Night

A lantern glows, a funny sight,
Dad dressed up, a big snow white.
Mom's sweater—ugly, yet it thrives,
Warmth and laughs, our love survives.

The cat wears antlers, what a mess,
Chasing lights, it's such distress.
We pluck the strings and sing out loud,
Even neighbors join the crowd!

Stockings hung with care and cheer,
Who ate the treat? The suspect's clear!
A bunny munches on the greens,
It's Christmas cheer, or so it seems.

As bedtime falls, the giggles swirl,
With tinsel hair, I give a twirl.
In the glow of glow-in-the-dark,
Love ignites the holiday spark.

Legacy of Kindness

A gift exchanged, a little prank,
With each giggle, we fill the tank.
Handmade cards, with crayon hearts,
Who knew giving warms the arts?

Silly sweaters, jokes, and cheer,
Laughter echoes, drawing near.
Bright lights twinkle on the tree,
Come join the fun, it's a spree!

A snowman wiggles, trying to dance,
Our family bonding, in a trance.
Take a moment, share a smile,
Kindness counts, it goes a mile.

From heart to heart, we pass delight,
In every hug, our spirits ignite.
The memories made, a true delight,
Laughter and love, our Christmas light.

Passing the Light

With candles lit, the shadows play,
Naughty jokes brighten the gray.
Pass the light, let laughter flow,
Twinkle toes in the glow.

The game of charades takes its turn,
Funny faces, watch them burn.
Each silly act, a shared delight,
Together we shine, what a sight!

Gift cards wrapped in comic style,
Pranks that make us laugh awhile.
Under the mistletoe, we grin,
With every smile, we let love win.

In all the cheer, we find our way,
Warmth and laughter, come what may.
Each story shared, a festive rite,
In the glow of love, we pass the light.

Gifts of Time: The Ultimate Offering

Tick-tock goes the clock, oh what a sight,
Wrapped up in laughter, we party all night.
Forget the expensive, just lend me your ear,
Your time is the treasure I hold most dear.

Jumping at duties, like kids on their train,
Building with laughter, it counteracts pain.
We'll race to the fridge for a snack or two,
Our only agenda? Just silly and new.

With each passing hour, giggles abide,
Socks as our weapons, we start the confide.
Share stories of clips that make no sense,
Time flies on wings, it's so immense!

So here's my suggestion, let's make a pact,
Our moments together are forever intact.
Instead of a gadget, or glitzy bauble,
Let's gift each other a silly guffawble.

Beneath the Stars: A Gesture of Kindness

Under the stars, we gather tonight,
With cupcakes and cookies, oh what a sight!
Whiskers the cat thinks he's part of the fun,
Dancing and prancing, he just wants to run.

A sandwich for you and a laugh for me,
Who knew that kindness would come with such glee?
We'll trade all our quirks, like old-timey men,
Sharing our secrets, again and again.

Stars will be jealous of our silly cheer,
As we craft our strange stories over the beer.
Let's raise some eyebrows with missions so sly,
Delivering giggles with each little lie.

Give me a chuckle, I'll return the favor,
Tales of wild antics, what fun they can savor!
Beneath the vast heavens, we'll leave it unspoken,
Return to our homes with our hearts never broken.

Fireside Chats and Heartfelt Gifts

Gather 'round the fire, my dear little friends,
With marshmallows handy and warmth that transcends.
A movie of flops plays silly and bright,
While we belly laugh 'til the morning light.

Socks on the shelf? What a curious sight!
They're hidden secrets that peek through the night.
We'll swap sweets and stories, a whimsical fight,
With each heartfelt giggle, our souls feel so light.

Chatter with grandma, her tales never stale,
Of penguins and oranges that danced without fail.
Let's cheer for our bloopers, both big and small,
In this cozy cabin, we know we stand tall.

As we bid adieu to the fire's warm glow,
We'll leave with our hearts all aglow,
For gifts that are woven with laughter and cheer,
Are nestled within us, all throughout the year.

The Artistry of Giving

With paintbrush in hand, I craft from my heart,
A gift like no other, a whimsical start.
An ugly sweater, a delightful jest,
The art of my giving is put to the test.

Handmade cards made from spaghetti and glue,
Each stroke is a giggle, a colorful hue.
Transformed mundane items, like banana peels,
Into treasures of laughter, oh how it feels!

Socks for your dog? What a marvelous find!
Fuzzy and silly, they'll put you in mind.
Let's shuffle and dance in our outlandish gear,
Our free-spirited nature, no need for a sphere.

So here's to the moments we cherish and share,
In this crazy life, we're stripped down and bare.
The artistry of giving comes wrapped with a grin,
Let's paint joy together, where shenanigans begin!

Nurturing the Spirit of Togetherness

Warm hats for snowmen, a sight to see,
They wear them proudly, just like you and me.
Socks on the reindeer, red and green,
Fashionable friends, a sight so keen.

Cookies for Santa, with sprinkles galore,
One tasted too many, now we hide by the door.
Milk spilling over, oh what a scene,
Our giggles and crumbs, simply serene.

Echoes of Laughter and Love

Gift-wrapping chaos, the tape's gone rogue,
Bows on our heads, in festive vogue.
Uncle Fred's sweater, two sizes too wide,
We can't help but laugh, with love as our guide.

Trees adorned with tinsel, a glittering sight,
But the cat's on a mission, ready to fight.
Down goes the garland, a flurry of fur,
This holiday spirit, it's quite the big blur.

Bundle of Good Deeds

Baking up treats but forgot the salt,
'Tastes like cardboard!' we laugh—it's our fault!
Gifts poorly wrapped, with odd holes too,
Each one a puzzle, what did we do?

Jingle bells ringing, but quite out of tune,
Dancing like crazy, under the moon.
Neighbors all smiling, and joining the fun,
Our joyful ruckus has only begun!

Starry Nights

Stars shining bright, but where's that light?
The bulbs are all tangled, oh what a fright!
Counting the presents, but oh what a mess,
Who brought the glitter? It's hard to guess.

Snowflakes a-fallin', angels in the snow,
With snowballs we gather, in laughter we throw.
Veering off course, a slippery slide,
Rolling on laughter, we joyfully glide.

Kind Hearts

The puppy in the box, what a surprise!
But now he's a menace, with twinkling eyes.
Chasing the stockings, oh what a thrill,
We find them, or rather, we never will!

Zany sweater parties, so funny indeed,
Wearing from grandma, sparked by a need.
Coming together, in laughter we cheer,
Our hearts are the gifts that keep drawing near.

Chasing Shadows with Light

Jingle bells and fruitcake dreams,
A cat in a box, or so it seems.
With tinsel tangled in my hair,
I spread my cheer, but where's my chair?

My cousin's gift was quite a fright,
A dancing Santa in neon light.
It flops and spins, it sings so loud,
I'm laughing hard, I'm so proud!

Gifts wrapped in paper, such a chore,
I swear I bought ten, but found just four.
The kids are giggling, what a thrill,
A box of socks—they want a grill!

Under the tree, what's that surprise?
A funny hat that's ten sizes wide.
We wear it proudly, for the fun,
This day, dear friends, we've clearly won!

A Tapestry of Shared Joy

Cookies baking, flour in the air,
Grandma's secret, a joke to share.
Burnt on one side, but we don't mind,
A taste of love is what we find!

Neighbors bartering for goodies sweet,
"My fudge for your pie, a tasty treat!"
The kids are bouncing, all aglow,
Tripping on toys, look out below!

A snowman made with mismatched socks,
A carrot nose from Dad's old box.
He tips and falls, a wobbly sight,
We laugh and shout, 'What a delight!'

With laughter ringing through the night,
We gather 'round, a cozy sight.
The joy we share, a gift most rare,
In silly moments, love is there!

Comfort in Kindred Spirits

Hot cocoa spills, oh what a mess,
My dog's got marshmallows on his dress.
He's hogging all the warmth tonight,
Normal shenanigans—what a sight!

The sweater I wore is two sizes too small,
But Auntie says it's the best of all.
With bells that jingle, it's quite the show,
I strut around, just let me glow!

Tales of past mishaps, we laugh and cheer,
Reliving moments that bring us near.
A broken ornament here or there,
Each laugh shared adds to our flair!

With friends who know just how to jest,
We revel together, feeling blessed.
In cozy corners, spirits lift,
The laughter shared—a treasured gift!

A Cascade of Goodwill

Look at the lights, they're tangled tight,
As I trip over the cord—what a sight!
The tree is leaning, it almost fell,
With a bit of giggles, all is well!

My buddy brought a fruitcake treat,
But one big slice could stop a fleet.
We joke and wince, it's hard to chew,
"Do you have water?" "Might need two!"

Presents piled high, one for the cat,
He snoozes away on my brother's hat.
With ribbons everywhere, what a scene,
Our wrap battle—truly unforeseen!

So here's to laughter, friendship and cheer,
With funny moments, the best time of year.
So pass the cookies and make a toast,
To silly times—those we love the most!

Starry Nights and Kind Deeds

Beneath the stars, we play our part,
With gifts of laughter, a joyful heart.
Santa's helpers, dressed in cheer,
Bringing smiles, spreading love near.

In snowflakes' dance, we find a way,
To share our joy on this fine day.
With cookies baked and ribbons tight,
Let's make each moment feel just right.

Mittens tossed and scarves on the floor,
Gifts are wrapped, oh, who wants more?
We sneak around, planning a prank,
The joy of giving, we shall not tank.

Under moonlight, we gather round,
With every laugh, pure joy is found.
In silly hats and bags of cheer,
We celebrate, spreading joy, my dear!

Nurturing the Flame of Compassion

In the kitchen, chaos blooms,
Pies with faces and dancing brooms.
Each spoonful served brings such delight,
The gift of warmth on a cool night.

Socks as gifts, oh what a sight,
Striped and polka-dotted, pure delight.
With giggles shared over clumsy ties,
We wrap our love in silly lies.

Around the fire, stories flow,
Of that one gift that stole the show.
With poking sticks and playful glee,
We nurture joy, you and me.

So toast to laughter, a toast to cheer,
With every hug that draws us near.
In our hearts, a flame does glow,
Nurtured by kindness, watch it grow!

In Every Box, a Piece of Light

Wrapped in paper, a treasure waits,
Funny faces and mismatched plates.
Each box hums with cheer inside,
Full of laughter, oh, what a ride!

A squeaky toy hides in plain sight,
For Grandma's cat, what a silly fright!
With bows on heads and tape on hands,
We craft our joy, as friendship expands.

The puzzles mixed, the game askew,
What's next in store? A dancing shoe!
In every corner, giggles spring,
Who knew a sock could be this bling?

With every gift, we share a spark,
In every box, a smiling mark.
As laughter rises, let's unite,
In every box, a piece of light!

Whispers of Joy in the Cold

In winter's chill, we find our way,
With mugs of cocoa, bright as day.
Laughter echoes, spirits soar,
As we gather tight, and give some more.

Snowmen made of mismatched socks,
Prancing around, in silly frocks.
With every snowball, a giggle flies,
Beneath this sky, goodwill lies.

With jingle bells and goofy hats,
We dance and shout, just like the cats.
In every corner, warmth unfolds,
Whispers of joy, like tales of old.

So wrap it up in love's embrace,
With silly dances, we find our place.
In every laugh beneath the cold,
Our hearts grow warm, our stories told.

Heartfelt Tokens of Thanks

A gift for you, so bright and sweet,
Wrapped up in paper, oh what a treat!
With ribbons and bows, a delightful show,
Unwrap my love, it's the best I know.

Your smile is gold, it makes me cheer,
Like cookies and milk, oh dear, oh dear!
A squeaky toy that wiggles with glee,
Join me in laughter, let's dance with glee!

When socks are the gift, don't pout or frown,
Just think of warm feet when skating in town!
With mittens so cozy, let's toast by the fire,
Sharing hot cocoa, it brings us up higher!

So here's to the joy, of giving with fun,
To friends and to family, let's spread it to everyone!
In every small gift, a story we weave,
Together in laughter, let's never leave!

Joyful Whispers of December

Tinsel draped high, on the tree it sways,
A gift from the cat that's chewed all the rays!
With sparkles and giggles, we hide little toys,
Even a sock for our rowdy boys!

In December warm hugs make the best delight,
And a fruitcake that bounces with every bite!
Who knew a "fruit" could be so absurd?
With a wink and a grin, let's share the word!

Gifts of the heart come wrapped in delight,
Like a dancing penguin that steals the night.
Together we giggle, we sing a sweet song,
In this room of warmth, where we all belong!

So gather your friends, let's toast to the cheer,
With snowballs of laughter, and good tidings near.
For under the stars, we'll create our moan,
In this jolly season, we never roam alone!

A Gift Wrapped in Warmth

A present for you, a penguin so bright,
With silly little legs, that dance through the night.
Wrapped up in fluff, it's snuggly and round,
You'll giggle so hard, it'll burst all around.

With cookies that crumble and sprinkles that glint,
I promise this gift won't make you squint!
A note in each package, drawn just like me,
With doodles and smiles, can you see the glee?

So get ready for hugs, and giggles galore,
With laughter and cheer, who could ask for more?
As ribbons unwind, let joy take its place,
These warm little tokens are filled with grace!

A fumble, a tumble, oh what a delight!
Gifts full of laughter always feel so right.
So let's raise our mugs and relish the cheer,
In a season of giving, I'm glad you are here!

Radiance Beneath the Evergreen

Beneath the tall tree, the ornaments shine,
With a cat chasing strings, oh isn't that fine?
A gift from the heart, wrapped up with care,
An old Christmas sweater with frills you can wear!

In cheerful delight, we share all our fun,
Like snowmen with hats who suddenly run!
With homemade delights that wobble and sway,
Let's toast to the laughter that brightens our day!

So gather 'round close, we'll share all our tales,
Of mishaps and gifts, and laughter that prevails.
In the glow of the lights, as cookies get munched,
We'll savor the joy, all together, we'll crunch!

So let's spread the cheer, like confetti in air,
For the warmth of this season is beyond compare.
With each thoughtful gesture, our spirits align,
In the magic of giving, our hearts intertwine!

Winter's Embrace of Sharing

Snowmen dance in silly hats,
Gifts wrapped in cats and bats.
Laughter echoes through the night,
As reindeer take off in flight.

Cookies tossed like snowflakes fall,
Elves tripping on their candy brawl.
Mittens fly through frosty air,
As we unwrap the fun to share.

Fires crackle, stories told,
Presents peek from bags of gold.
Everyone dons their jolly grin,
And giggles spill like spiced-up gin.

In this warmth, hearts come alive,
From silly pranks, we all derive.
As winter whispers in our ear,
We spread the cheer, oh so dear.

A Sprinkle of Joy for Every Soul

Socks are hung with too much care,
One gremlin steals—was it a bear?
With tinsel tangled in our hair,
We laugh 'til breath is hard to share.

Pies that wobble like a deer,
A dog that's chewed the gift this year.
Everyone's giggling, no room for tears,
As we belt out those silly cheers.

Chasing down the greedy loot,
Wrapped boxes housing a big ol' hoot.
Magic moments brought with glee,
While uncle bursts a button or three.

Oh what fun to give and take,
With playful gags, there's no mistake.
In this season, joy's the goal,
With laughter brightening every soul.

Threads of Light: The Ties That Bind

Ornaments made from old shoelaces,
Tangled up in goofy places.
We dance around the twinkling lights,
With goofy grins that give such flights.

Wrapping paper like a puzzle,
Ties entwined in festive muzzle.
We play the game and act so sly,
As gifts seem to levitate and fly.

Laughter's the bow on every gift,
Even when we're sure we'll drift.
A tie of joy, a wink, a glance,
We all are pulled into this dance.

With silly hats atop our heads,
We share our hearts, not just our breads.
In every fold, a memory finds,
The threads of light the season binds.

Echoes of Laughter and Love

Frosty windows, peek-a-boo,
'Til the carolers sing us through.
Giggles ring from every side,
As we splash in puddles, mouths wide.

The mistletoe? A clumsy trap,
Where Auntie fumbles and takes a nap.
Gifts exchanged, some odd and bright,
Tickling ribs with every light.

Magic sprinkles in the air,
Puppies prance without a care.
With every hug, we grow so bold,
And share our stories, bright and old.

Echoes bounce off walls of cheer,
With every gift, we hold so dear.
In joy and laughter, we find our way,
Painting bright memories this holiday.

The Canvas of Generosity

In a town where snowmen wear hats made of cheese,
Gift-giving started to spread like a breeze.
A reindeer in boots danced down the lane,
While jolly old elves sang songs of the rain.

A cat in a scarf snoozed under the tree,
With a bowl full of fish quite pleased as can be.
The gifts piled high, all wrapped up with flair,
One gift rolled away, but no one did care.

A box filled with socks and a pair of old shoes,
Brought laughter and giggles, no time for the blues.
With a wink and a smile, they shared all their treats,
A holiday feast with some strange other sweets.

So gather around, with your friends near and dear,
With kindness and laughter, spread joy and good cheer.
For in the giving, hilarity thrives,
Like a snowman in flip-flops, so funny and wise.

Moments of Magic and Reflection

In a kitchen where gingerbread houses spread wide,
Cookies were stolen, oh what a fun ride!
With icing and sprinkles stuck all in the hair,
They laughed till they cried, without a single care.

A snowball fight broke out, kids dodging with glee,
One snowy-eyed dog then joined in the spree.
A mittens' mishap sent snowflakes to flight,
As we've learned—a good slapstick can tickle all night.

Laughter erupted as Grandpa let slip,
A secret about an elf and a potato chip.
Unruly and chubby, they jumped into cheer,
Toasting to friendships, and maybe some beer!

So here's to the moments, both silly and bright,
In the spirit of giving, everything feels right.
For sharing a laugh is the best gift we own,
Like a punchline in socks, it's joy fully grown.

Enchanted by Acts of Kindness

A partridge popped out with a wink and a grin,
He saw the tale of kindness where all would begin.
A tree fully loaded with gifts—a delight,
Even the cat joined to create the night's light.

Neighbors threw parties with leftover fruitcake,
One slice was a weapon! It made quite a quake.
With laughter infectious and juggling a pie,
Even the turkey gave thanks with a sigh.

They wrapped up a goat in the finest of bows,
Which turned out to nibble on everyone's toes.
But kindness won over amid all the jest,
As everyone hugged and declared it the best.

In heartwarming chaos, love found its own way,
Through funny mishaps that made everyone stay.
So let's share our moments, our giggles, and fun,
For gifts bring us closer, and laughter's a home run!

Togetherness Under the Holiday Sky

Beneath a grand sky full of twinkling lights,
Families gathered for hilarious sights.
With mittens and scarves, and a dog in a hat,
They launched colorful snowballs and laughed at the spat.

The glow of the fire warmed all through the night,
As stories were shared, oh what a delight!
Mom's pie hit the ceiling while it wobbled with care,
"Next year we bake, but first, let's beware!"

With hot cocoa flowing and spirits so high,
Pinecones and laughter were tossed to the sky.
A dance with the broom led to giggles galore,
While Aunt Emily's wig found a path to the floor.

In moments like these, as the snowflakes all tumbled,
The joy of togetherness kept them all jumbled.
So lift up your voices, your hearts, and your cheer,
For sharing this magic brings all we hold dear.

Illuminated by Generosity

Lights twinkle and gleam, oh what a sight,
Under the tree, the gifts pile up tight.
A cat in a box, claiming it as its own,
While we exchange socks, instead of a throne.

Laughter erupts with each silly hat,
As Uncle Joe's mustache gets stuck on the cat.
Mistletoe hanging, but no one's aware,
Of Grandma's bad aim as she throws out a chair.

Yet in all the chaos, we gather and share,
Best cookies from Betty, no one could compare.
With buzzing excitement, we tear and we cheer,
Office supplies as gifts? Well, never fear!

By evening our hearts, they are full and aglow,
With laughter and kindness, we let our love flow.

A Symphony of Care

The choir of joy, where giggles abound,
Ringing laughter is our favorite sound.
We try to sing carols, but oh, what a mess,
Grandpa's off-key, we just can't suppress!

The turkey's a monster, we swear it could bite,
And Aunt Edna's salad? A questionable sight.
The gifts start to fly, as we toss in the air,
I've wrapped up a broom, and everyone's aware!

The tree's overview looks like a tornado,
Tinsel hair on the dog, what a great show!
But in all the madness, one thing shines through,
It's the love we all feel, just being with you.

So let's raise a glass to this whimsical night,
Each chuckle and grin is a true heart's delight.

Moments Wrapped in Joy

Gather around, let the fun unfold,
With stories of mishaps and laughter retold.
The kids have gone wild, they're sugar-fueled sprinters,
While Dad loses track of his ghost pepper dinner.

The wrapping paper battles in every hand,
As each one declares their valuable brand.
A fish-shaped sweater is one grandma's fate,
And socks on the cat? Yes, she's now first rate!

Sneaking up snacks, we're masters of stealth,
With cookies and milk, we nourish our health.
But then comes the slip, oh no! Down they go,
Like tumbleweeds rolling, our smiles overflow.

Through moments so silly, the clock hits the night,
In happiness woven, we hold each other tight.

Unfolding the Gift of Presence

Under the mistletoe, chaos just reigns,
Someone's misplaced all the cranberry canes.
Kids are unwrapped like toys on the floor,
As we contemplate who wants a new door!

With gloved hands, we tackle this blizzard of cheer,
While Aunt Sue's knitting leads us to fear.
Her sweater's a riot, with stripes that collide,
But her love overshadows any fashion slide.

Grandma brings cookies, with questionable taste,
As we all volunteer to help clear the space.
Yet under the laughter, it's clear as can be,
The greatest of gifts is just you and me.

So let's toast to the season, we frantically share,
With joy in abundance, and love in the air.

A Symphony of Generosity

In the kitchen, chaos reigns,
Cookies burning, oh, what pains!
Gift wrap flying, tape on the floor,
A cat in the box? Who could ask for more!

With tangled lights and misfit toys,
We giggle loud, no room for poise.
Laughter echoes, the spirit's bright,
Oh, what fun on this silly night!

A neighbor drops by, holding a pie,
But the dog snatches it—oh me, oh my!
We share the crumbs, now slightly less,
"Next year, more planning, let's do our best!"

So raise a glass, with cocoa to sip,
Toast to the joy of friendship's trip.
This time of year, it's plain to see,
Chaos and laughter—a symphony!

The Glow of Kindness Unwrapped

A present awaits, but what's inside?
Is it socks or a game? Let's take a ride!
The paper tears with great delight,
I never knew I needed a kite!

With jingle bells that don't quite ring,
We dance about, as we awkwardly sing.
The tree's a beacon, all lit and bright,
But the cat thinks it's her own delight!

Pine needles dropped like glittering rain,
Underfoot they crackle, oh, what a pain!
Yet in all the mess, there's glee to find,
Surrounded by laughter, all hearts aligned.

So here's to the joy, the smells and tastes,
With little mishaps, we won't let waste.
We cherish the quirks, they make us grin,
This time of year, let the fun begin!

Twinkling Lights of Compassion

Twinkling lights on the house next door,
They blink and sizzle—who needs decor?
The garland's tangled, the wreath's askew,
 But we laugh until we can't see through!

Cookies and laughs fit our delight,
 Flour on the face—a snowy sight.
"Who knocked the tree?" we all inquire,
 Oh dear, was that a cat or a choir?

We sip on cider, a spicey brew,
 Debating fruitcake; can it be true?
But in the clinks of our mugs and chips,
We toast to the year with hilarious quips.

So gather 'round, let the stories flow,
 Each silly tale adds to the show.
In the heart of laughter, we see it clear—
It's the joy we share that brings us cheer!

Echoes of Joy in Every Gesture

The season's here, let's raise a cheer,
For socks and ties and every weird beer!
Neighbors popping over with treats to share,
While our old dog snoozes without a care.

Mismatched sweaters, a fashion faux pas,
But it's the love that shines, hurrah!
Wrapped up giggles in shiny wraps,
While Aunt Edna spills her tea—what a lapse!

Gift cards or socks? What's the surprise?
"Just don't give me the fruitcake," she sighs.
We're all just weirdos, each one a gem,
Celebrating quirks with a loud diadem.

So let's crank the tunes, dance without grace,
Embracing the chaos, a warm embrace.
In this wonderland not made of gold,
It's the joy of the moment and stories told!

Wrapped in Love: A Holiday Tale

I wrapped a gift in silly paper,
Thinking it would be a caper.
But when they unwrapped, what did they see?
A pair of socks, not quite for me!

I tried to bake some holiday treats,
But ended up with chocolate beats.
Now every bite is just for show,
Cardboard cookies, oh what a woe!

My cat got lost in bows and tape,
Now he's dressed as Santa—what a shape!
He prances 'round like he knows the score,
While I chase him down for a snack or more.

The joy we share, oh what a sight,
Laughter echoes through the night.
With goofy smiles and jolly cheer,
We'll make this season full of beer!

Beneath the Boughs: A Gift of Time

Under the branches, I found a surprise,
A gift from Uncle, much to my demise.
It was a clock that runs backward, you see,
Now I'm never late for family tea!

We played a game called "what's in the sack?"
With odds and ends, it was quite the whack.
A rubber chicken and a shoe, oh my!
Who knew the laughter would reach the sky?

A sweater knitted with two left hands,
Looks like it was made by clowning bands.
Yet I wear it with pride on this day,
Fashion's not perfect, but it's here to stay!

With stories shared and giggles galore,
Each silly moment opens a door.
Time spent together is the finest rhyme,
As we bask in the glow of our own sweet time!

Festival of Giving Hearts

In a garish sweater, I danced with glee,
Gift-wrapped a joke, but where's the esprit?
A singing fish, it flops with style,
Who knew a laugh could go a mile?

We held a contest for best gift wrap,
But all I got was a dog's big nap.
With bows in the air, it flew across,
Turns out the winner was just a toss!

A fruitcake flew, it made a grand splash,
Landed on Uncle Bob—what a crash!
He smiled with crumbs stuck on his face,
Nothing says joy like a cake-throwing race!

So here's to the quirks that bring us cheer,
We'll treasure the folly, year after year.
In this merry tale, let's raise a toast,
To laughter and fun, that's what we love most!

Bright Spirits on Dark Winter Days

On gloomy days, we spread the cheer,
With silly hats and a mug of beer!
A penguin suit was my gift to Paul,
Now he waddles through the mall.

We made snowmen with funny faces,
One fell over—oh, what the chases!
With carrots for noses and laughs so bright,
That's a gift done just right!

I tried to sing a carol, so sweet,
But tripped on my tongue, what a feat!
Yet everyone laughed and clapped with glee,
Guess this odd version was best for me!

With wrapped-up giggles in every heart,
We'll cherish these memories, a true work of art.
So when winter gets cold and starts to sway,
Let's spread fun and joy in a zany way!

Gifts from the Heart

A box of socks, the perfect find,
With stripes and spots that blow your mind.
A rubber chicken, all squeaky and bright,
Wrapped up tight, oh what a sight!

A fruitcake shaped like a flying bat,
"I baked this fresh!" but it's really flat.
But laughter dies when gifts go wrong,
We'll belt out carols and sing along!

Mittens for cats, a fuzzy delight,
They'll throw a tantrum, oh what a fight!
A coupon for hugs, one size fits all,
We'll share a giggle at the winter ball!

So pass the joy, all wrapped in cheer,
'Tis the season, so hold your dear.
With laughter and whimsy, we light the way,
To gifts from the heart, come what may!

Merry Tidings of Grateful Souls

A sweater knitted with love but so frayed,
It looks like it was run over by a parade.
With patterns so wild, it's totally fine,
We'll wear it proudly, it's one of a kind!

A jar of pickle juice, oh what a feat,
"Drink this," it says, "it's a tasty treat!"
Others may snicker, but we'll just smile,
This joyful gift will go the extra mile!

A baffling puzzle with missing parts,
"It's still a challenge!" as buying starts.
Together we'll piece our lives with care,
Grateful for laughter, so sweet and rare!

In every odd gift, we find delight,
Each chuckle shared shines oh so bright.
Merry moments, they make us whole,
With merry tidings from grateful souls!

The Magic of Shared Smiles

A rubber duck in a Santa hat,
Quacking joy, imagine that!
It floats through the air with cheer so grand,
Spreading laughter across the land!

A fruitcake that's gifted one too many times,
"Oh you shouldn't have," but it still chimes!
We'll cut it open, maybe a surprise,
A hidden treasure in muffin disguise!

Wacky socks that beep and flash,
Each step a giggle, oh what a clash!
Sharing them round, a jolly parade,
Happy feet dancing, plans we've made!

The spark of joy when our eyes align,
In shared smiles and gifts, our hearts combine.
With magic moments stirred like a stew,
We find pure bliss in all that we do!

Spirit of the Season in Every Act

A gift card for ice cream that never expires,
It sparks up joy and fuels our desires.
With flavors like pickle and garlic delight,
We'll scoop and we'll laugh with all our might!

An inflatable reindeer to adorn the lawn,
It dances and twirls from dusk until dawn.
Neighbors all chuckle, and join in the fun,
The spirit of joy, shining like sun!

A handmade card with crayons and flair,
"You're my best buddy!" it boldly declares.
Taking turns crafting, it's messy but bright,
The laughter we share is pure, pure light!

In every small act, a joy we can glean,
From baking to sharing and all in between.
The spirit of the season's in every small act,
With love and some humor, it's a perfect pact!

Milton Keynes UK
Ingram Content Group UK Ltd.
UKHW021111181124
451360UK00015B/1285